Mois Benarroch

Copyright © 2018
Home Bayit
ISBN: 9781728810928
Mois Benarroch
Cover: Matteo Losurdo & Liah Benarroch

All rights reserved.

No part of this publication may be reproduced or transmitted in any form or by any means, mechanical or electronic, including photocopying or recording, or by any information storage and retrieval system, or transmitted by email without permission in writing from the publisher.

HOME

Home Bayit
 was

TRANSLATED FROM THE HEBREW BY
ROCHELLE MASS.

"I burned the best book I ever wrote the moment it was finished. It was perfect, it couldn't be improved, I can still see it in front of my eyes, the smoke rising from it, reminding me that the book that exists is as valuable as the one that no longer exists."

(Paulus The Sad ... "Memories of Pancho Del Toro", as quoted by Menashe Har Esh, in his book "HOME".)

The first time I heard about the book 'HOME' was when I was five years old, my father showed it to me proudly: "One day you will read this book." I answered him as proudly: "I will write it!" He yelled and reminded me that just the year before I had said to him: "Father, write Bialik's poems for me" after I had heard Bialik's poetry for the first time in the kindergarten. My father was a future poet. He had written maybe five poems, however, he always talked about the big book of poetry he was about to write. He would come home every year with a new car, saying: "My son", he never called me by name, "this is a new car, but truthfully I would rather write a book of poetry than write a new car, buy a new car, for it is only matter, you understand, and matter goes, it conquers you, controls you." The years passed and following the period referred to as the "Shopping Spree" he seemed very sad because we owned the same car for more than ten years, even rides were few because there was a scarcity of both fuel and coupons from the government, few spare parts and not much money.

He could talk for hours about the book, for an entire year that's almost all he talked about, even though I was only six years old I understood that the book dealt with the connection between parents and children, the home, the importance of the woman in the home, about the end of the century, the end of the millennium, about the loss of love.

"There's no love in the world", he told my mother one morning, and started a great philosophical discussion about love through the centuries, "Just like Har Esh says, Menashe Har Esh, in his book HOME — and so on, without end, talking in words I couldn't understand.

Years later I heard about the book from my girlfriend Michelle when I was fifteen. She also talked about it with the same astonishment and wonder, as others did later. However, what surprised me was that she seemed to be referring to another book altogether. She said that this book was about a journey to India in which the narrator, David Malchi, goes to find his roots and returns to Judaism. I remember, for sure, that was the last time I ever saw the book. I saw the jacket, the picture of the camel, however, from my childhood memories and my father, I had adamantly refused to read it. My father's words: "One day you will read it" continued to echo in my head, then my answer: "You won't decide for me what I'll do and what I won't, I'll decide for myself, if I decide not to, it'll not be what you want Father, especially not what you want."

Years passed. HOME was forgotten, I began to write books of poetry and then novels. From time to time someone would mention Menashe Har Esh as a poet and somewhat strange author on the margins of Hebrew literature who published four books as well as another that no one had even seen a copy of for at least ten years. This was, of course, HOME . I'm about to tell you the story of the search. From time to time a visitor would quote a few lines of the book from memory, or mention it, or describe the plot. Each reader, of course, remembered another story line.

Not only did I decide to look for a copy of the book, I also wanted to read it.

As my father said, his words took on another meaning after the birth of my two daughters. They became softer, a sort of stroking of memory during difficult moments. No doubt we are living in difficult times.

The first person I went to see was his son, Yoel Har Esh, a famous Homeopath in Jerusalem. It seemed that he had been waiting for years for the moment someone would ask about his father. "Twenty or twenty—five years ago, it's hard to say with the new calendar, he disappeared. I was thirteen years old, after my Bar Mitzvah, I'm sure, thirteen. The book, HOME, was in my possession, but after he disappeared I threw it out, with the dedication and everything. I was very angry with him. Perhaps I understand more today. He was very closed, loved very dearly on the one hand, suffered a great deal, as a child, from his father. You know that Homeopathy distinguishes between personality types. Today I understand and maybe because of it I went to study Homeopathy. I wanted to learn about my father and myself, he was a Natrum Muriaticum type, one who seems relaxed, seems to deal well with his environment, but keeps it all inside him. One day they just get up and go to live in some deserted village, they don't talk to anyone, they're completely alone.

"Without a doubt he deeply suffered from lack of literary success since he had invested all his resources in that, and the responses were so minimal. He talked a great deal about HOME, said that this was his greatest creation. He probably wrote it when I was seven years old, in school, he printed the book himself, brought it to me with a personal dedication. I don't remember what he wrote, I really don't know, something about a house, maybe, the family, a family book, he talked a lot about his own father, a little about his mother, it seemed the book was printed in only a few copies, maybe a hundred, maybe two hundred, no more than that."

"Didn't you look through it? Didn't you read it?"

"It wasn't exactly a children's book. Maybe here and there I read a few pages, I didn't understand much, it was written in very complicated language, certainly not for children, he talked a great deal about the book, then one day he stopped, just like everything else he did. He would talk about one subject for months, for years, then you wouldn't hear a thing about it, he would go onto another subject, to astrology or homeopathy, then would write a book, then would talk about the book he was writing and nothing else, and then onto something else, like Kabbalah. All the time it was another topic, then one day he'd stop talking about it, and one day he completely stopped speaking and disappeared. My mother never understood, she died two years after he disappeared.

"And your sister?"

"My older sister died two years ago. In the year 66 B.E.D., Before the End of Days. If I'm not mistaken, that is how they counted the years till the End if Days. It's sort of confusing."

"They added a year."

"Oh, yes, you're right, they added a year, so it is 66, but anyway it was two years ago, maybe her children have the book, maybe her oldest, he must be about twenty now, but my sister lived in New York. I don't know where her son lives; she was much older than me, so there wasn't much connection between us."

"Friends?"

"He had a friend who is still living; he's a lecturer at the University, Goldstein. Professor Goldstein. He's really the only one, I think, that teaches a course about him. He didn't have many friends, he was always busy writing. Tell me, why are you looking for this book?"

"It's a long story, it's connected with my father. He would show me the book all the time, he was very contented of it, and told me that one day I would read it, a childhood memory. A memory that persecutes me."

"A strong father, a difficult father ... I understand."

"Can I come and talk with you if I have more questions?"

He didn't answer. The next day I went to see Prof. Goldstein at the University on Mount Scopus. Prof. B. Goldstein was written on the door.

"You must have come to talk with me about an important subject. It's dangerous to come here, I haven't left the building for years, they're shooting everywhere."

"Shooting?"

"Yes, I don't know where people live, each time I poke my head out the window I see a bomb lying over there."

"Menashe Har Esh. The House."

"Menashe Har Esh? No one ever asked me about him, what brings you to ask about Menashe Har Esh? And, about The House. This book is essentially fictitious, it has not been written. Har Esh spoke about it, even published a few copies of that name on his own account, but these were chapters from other books, a sort of collage. I am not even sure that it was published. I never saw a copy."

I look at him sternly, and said, to him, without reason: "You are lying!"

"I'm lying?"

His face showed that he hesitated to

admit he was lying or that he wanted to throw me out of his office.

"He was my good friend and a very talented author. He wrote seven books, a cycle of seven in the life of the world, or something like that. Each book was to be one of the seven planets revolving around the sun, one of the fast planets, also one of the days of the week, and other symbols. It was a failure, that is, the man worked on the project for more than twenty years, and it failed in literary and economic terms. He believed in his books. I told him to write a book a little more open symbolically, a little more communicative and he brought me 'HOME'. I fell apart when I saw the manuscript. It was madness. At that time it was suicide to talk about the holy temple in Hebrew literature. Maybe even now I don't know, it was literary suicide on a large scale, that's what he called it. He would have committed suicide every day, Menashe, he said to me, I remember his words exactly: 'Baruch — these words are in the air, I don't choose them, they come to me, they land on my pages.' I thought this was absolutely nonsense. Derida also said that there are things that must be written and someone simply does it. That's the way he justified Nazi articles by his teacher and that's the way he was able to justify his philosophy of life, you understand. Someone has to write it, and so it's written. Where is freedom of choice? He was very angry with my criticism and since then our relationship cooled a great deal. I haven't seen a copy of the book, however I heard that he printed a limited series of HOME. I don't know if this is right or not, I am not able to tell you, but I think it's true."

Suddenly I remembered his name, Baruch Goldstein, I'd heard it before.

"Baruch Goldstein, do you know where your name comes from?"

"My father was called Gold. He was born in the United States, seemed this was an abbreviation of Goldenberg, but there was a just man called Goldstein and so he changed his name to Goldstein, gave me the name of the Baruch Goldstein, the Just. I really don't know what he did, but there are people that go to visit his grave. I have never gone there. I don't believe in graves. I don't even go to Razin's grave.

"I heard that Baruch Goldstein was a criminal, that he'd go into Arab homes and murder the husband, then rape the wife. Something like that. Sort of a Jessie James of the Wild East. I don't know what's true and what's not. They also say that he murdered a Minister during the War for Peace."

"The War of Peace? I haven't yet heard about that war. I don't know anything about this Baruch Goldstein and I have no interest in him. The past is so confusing, the present isn't anything special. I have been sleeping here for the last two years. I haven't left the building. My home was ruined."

THE HAND OF CIRCUMSTANCE

Two weeks later I took a walk through Nahalat Shiva, on Yasser Street. Suddenly I felt a hand on my back. A big man with a white glove stood behind me and talked so quickly that he swallowed half his words. "I'vegothe book thatyoure lookinfor."

"How do you know that I'm looking for a book?"

"Iknow... comewithme."

I went along, trying to keep up with his pace. We came to the place, through Gan Oslo, to Ya'acov Razin Boulevard, then to Aza Street. All the way he talked.

"Youknowwho Ya'acovRazinwas? He was a very wise man from Morrocco who was murdered by Arabs in the uprisings of 1929 in Tel Aviv. A very just man, and now, every first of the month of Heshvan there is a celebration for the Babba Razin, did you know that?"

"I heard about it, but I don't like crowds."

"Everyone cries and lights candles, there are always people that go to visit the grave on Mount Razin to light candles. He was a very just man, so on the day of the festivities people buy lots of things they don't need so as to improve the economy of Israel. This is a very important act, buying as much as possible, especially when there is a celebration for a just men, like the Babba Razin, and also for the Rebbe Yehuda Perski Shalitah. His street is over there, not far. You have to return to the faith, David."

"How do you know my name?"

"I dreamt about it. Besides, I dreamt that one day you would be the King of Israel."

"Ah ha! King of Israel. Is there really something like that? We already have King Hassan, he is the king of the entire country, isn't he?"

"Never. We've arrived."

We went into a house without

electricity or television. In the corner of the room sat a child of about twelve years old, smiled at me and sang: "My father told me the messiah will come tomorrow."

"Sit down here for a minute. I have the book for you. Here it is."

The book was completely stuck together, perhaps from the heavy humidity that filled the house. HOME was written on the cover, without any mention of the author. The first page was faded, however it was possible to read the dedication 'to my friend Professor Goldstein' more or less clearly. And it was possible to understand something on page 48: "Your Honor, the Judge ... my apologies, Your Honor, I never said that I agree with murder, however, I am happy that this individual was murdered, I am happy since I didn't like him. I am also happy that my father died, since he left me a large inheritance. If every person who derives pleasure from the fact that someone has died is put in jail, you'd have to put half of the country into jail. King David organized a banquet after his son Absalom died, didn't he?"

What came after was all faded, pages were stuck one to the other.

"Home, Home. My holy Temple. I

weep for its destruction, I am already weeping for your construction, dead stones, many Rabbis, ... dark and hollow, once again the same lack of understanding, I weep for the destruction and you..." again faded.

"But," I said to him, "How do I know that this is the book? The name of the author does not appear anywhere. How do I know that this is Menashe Har Esh's book and not a book of the same name of someone else. Maybe according to the dedication, however, I would guess that many people have dedicated books to a professor of literature."

"This is the book and this is the house."

"Can I buy it from you?"

"No, I am not selling it."

I thought that this was a form of bargaining so as to get more money, but soon enough I realized that I was mistaken.

"I am ready to give you 200 zuzim."

"You make me laugh. What can you do with 200 zuzim?"

"What's happened to you? That's apartment rent for a year."

"I already have an apartment."

And the child began singing something again about salvation and the messiah. It seemed that this is what they talked about all the time.

"You should know that this is an important book for encouraging the coming of the Messiah. They say that whoever has it in his home when Ben David arrives will be the first to visit the Temple with him. There are maybe another ten people who have this book. Maybe less. However, no more than seventy people, that's for sure. This book is worth more than my house."

"Tell me, what is the dedication to Professor Goldstein?"

"Baruch Goldstein, the wicked, beastly one, who makes generations of students crazy, and pushes them to go from Judaism to the the State religion…, State religion… We didn't expect that even in the holy writings. I don't know why he dedicated the book to him, in any event I never bought it from him, rather a woman ... after her husband's death, who lived not far from my house. She's also passed away in the meantime."

I continued turning the pages of the book while we talked, and the pages began to separate, something which didn't make the reading any easier. It was possible to read a sentence here and a sentence there, but I wasn't sure that this was the book, and the more I read things seemed very far from the book that I was looking for.

"Thank you", I said. "You were a great help to me."

"Go on your way, don't be afraid, David. The day will come when you'll rule Israel, don't lose your way."

"The Jerusalem Syndrome," I said to myself and left his house.

I ran to Mount Scopus to meet with the professor. I found the University closed. People were running in the hallways, bringing tables, chairs and books.

"What's happening here?"

A pleasant woman who looked like a guide in the confusion said: "The University is closing. In its place the Observer Yeshiva will be erected."

"A Yeshiva?"

"A reform Yeshiva. The University is closing down because of a chronic lack of funds. It should not be forgotten that more than half of the Jewish population in Jerusalem is reform."

"I didn't know that."

" It's a fact."

"I'm looking for Professor Goldstein."

"I don't think you will be able to find him. Everyone left quite disappointed. They won't be returning. It was sudden. We bought the place through a tender ... an auction. "

"I'm looking for a book by Menashe Har Esh.

Someone walked quickly by and suddenly stopped.

"Menashe Har Esh? Is that what you said? Did you say Menashe Har Esh? ...You must be looking for HOME."

"Yes, Yes."

I went over, walked along quickly with him.

"Why are you looking for this book?"

"I really don't know. A childhood memory."

"Yes, you really look too young to know."

"To know what?"

"About 'HOME'... listen, I did research work on it ten years ago, maybe you can find it in the library. I had four copies of the book, and now I don't have even one. They tend to disappear then turn up in strange places. Try second hand stores.

"What is the book about?"

"This is the question of my research. Look, each one of the copies was different from the other. They all had the same name, without the author's name. I can't tell you about the entire research, but it seems that the author intended to write a book whose pages were printed by a cheap laser, each copy was to be different from the others, each reader would find the copy that is right for him, from a hypothesis which seems almost mystical to us today, based on a theory which claims that nothing in life is accidental, that everything eventually falls into place."

"I don't understand."

"It means that for each book there is one reader. I don't know how many copies were printed. They talked about dozens, maybe hundreds, maybe even thousands."

"The copies you had, what were they about?"

"It's hard for me to answer that. Maybe it was a political book, maybe mystical, a detective novel, a theological journey, philosophy, maybe all of these together, maybe none of them ... but I have a suggestion for you: look for the woman, perhaps she will lead you to what you are searching for. "

"What?"

"Always, when you look for something, look for the woman beyond the matter. Maybe his wife, maybe he had a lover or girlfriend at that time, but when you find the book, you can be assured that it's the only one of its kind, I would even say to you, don't search for the book, if a copy is to come to you, it'll come."

"I did see one copy but the pages were stuck together."

"Maybe in your search you are stuck on a mistaken idea?"

"What an idea! It's only a book that my father showed me when I was five years old."

"Think about it, maybe there are other reasons for your search, it isn't enough that your father showed it to you when you were five. There are other books your father showed you when you were five, and you're not looking for the others, there are many books in general ... more than enough."

B

"Mr. Sananes," the editor said to me, "This is a good article, but there are many mistakes. For a new journalist you are promising. What I don't understand is what is really happening in Jerusalem?"

"I don't know," I told him, "I don't know, it's as if there is no reality, as if everything happens yet nothing happens, you don't know who you will meet. Jerusalemites, most of them, feel like they are living under siege. They don't leave the city, even though there is no danger. I don't know what they are frightened of. It is as if each of them is wrapped in a bubble that represents their world, each world being different. They do not meet one another, there are those who think that peace has come to the country. Others think that war has broken out everywhere."

"And the book?"

"The book ..."

"HOME."

"I didn't find it. I even asked my father and he didn't remember the book, he is seventy years old, however, he talked about it for years. I don't understand what happened to that book."

"And the woman?"

"Fine, thank—you."

"No, I mean Menashe Har Esh's woman and Menashe Har Esh, is he still alive?"

"I think that he's still living, but I don't know how to find him and his book. I go around second hand shops. Maybe it's a matter of luck, or the opposite."

"When will you return?"

"Return where?"

"To Jerusalem."

"I'm not coming back. One more week there and I'll go crazy. If I'm staying there. I don't believe that a person can leave after a month. People loose their identity there. I have a friend who moved to Jerusalem and when I saw him, he wasn't the same person. He simply turned into a person from the past, changed his name. It was like talking into space. He was someone else, his way of speaking changed. No, I'm not going back, enough."

"You must return. I am going to publish your story, I'll announce that it will continue next month, in the next edition, if you want to continue working here, you better continue working."

He didn't say Shalom.

WITH HIS WIFE AT HOME

"Leave that work alone. You will always be able to find another job, you don't have to go back there."

"Newspapers are closing all the time, this is the best paper in Modi'in."

Every time David was pressured he would begin talking about his family.

"My grandfather came to Israel from Morocco."

"That's it. Begin with your grandfather."

"My grandfather's grandfather traveled his whole life, worked in Brazil, returning every few years to his home and his wife. That's how he made three children, came home then went back to Brazil, earned money."

"I never heard about him."

"Maybe I have family in Brazil. Afterwards, Moshe Sananes, or more correct, Mois Sananes, also wanted to go to Argentina. They offered him management of a Milk Marketing Company, his wife and mother cried and cried. They knew what would be waiting for them if he went, he canceled the whole thing at the last minute. You know, I can see him holding his suitcases, then actually putting them down on the floor and staying in Morocco, in his city, in Benshawen. I can see myself doing that. My grandfather came to Israel and broke down, he said, all the time that he was discriminated against because of his name, because he was from Morocco, he sacrificed his life, or at least that's what he said, so that his son could live in a Jewish country, that's my father, who came to Israel when he was 12 years old. He talked with me about discrimination all the time, but he gave birth to me when he was 55 years old. He always talked to me about what would have happened if he had gone to Paris, Madrid, New York, London like all his cousins who became successful. He talked only about those who succeeded. He was everywhere, except for the place in which he was, just like me."

"How is this connected with Jerusalem?" asked his wife and picked up the two month old baby so as to nurse her.

"It is has nothing to do with it, or it is all connected with it, my grandfather's dreams of Jerusalem, I want to feel that I belong to something, suddenly to something continuous, after I changed my name from Sananes to Koresh, I want to know where I come from and where I'm going to. Surely my father suffered when I changed my name, even now I don't talk to him a lot, and he doesn't speak. He hasn't spoken for five years. Maybe my son will change his name, look for his roots, I don't know, but I have to go to Jerusalem."

"It's dangerous there."

"Dangerous, not dangerous, maybe it's the safest place. A place of contrast, a place of God."

"God? ... are you talking about God?"

"My father talked a great deal about God, about the Temple, the Messiah, then he forgot. He forgot everything. I would also like to forget everything, to go into my brain just like a computer, and erase everything."

"David, I am afraid that you are going to Jerusalem."

She hugged him and he pushed her away.

"I am going to walk a little around Mt. Har Afat. I'll think more clearly about everything."

It was late afternoon. On the way to the mountain David passed the second hand book store of David Fogel, a sort of kind grandfather who knew how to talk about books with everyone. In the store there was a loud conversation about two typing errors in a book. "It can't be," the man said pointing so that David could also see, "Here, look, on page 110, WULD is written instead of WOULD. Did you see that? Maybe he wrote that intentionally, since Paul Aster would talk 5 pages later about the egg, I simple don't believe that Penguin Publishers would make a mistake like that, and in such a famous book as the New York Trilogy."

"The Egg?" asked the seller.

"There's another error. On page 157, instead of the letter a, □ appears, but maybe this is the Greek alphabet. This is very confusing. I can't find any reason for looking at it. How can we accept something like this, and from the Penguin Press, in particular. In this age of 999 computers and Tohu theory...."

"You know," said the seller, ignoring his new customers, "this book is based on the Theory of Chaos, a somewhat primitive theory concerning the relationship between distant events that was widely accepted fifty or sixty years ago, a rather humorous theory that essentially has brought about the economic downfall of the United States when they tried to implement it in economic terms. I think of so many theories that caused the disintegration of governments and wars that I say to myself that now when we are following theories of Tohu maybe we will also ruin ourselves, the strongest economy in the world."

The man looked at me and I noticed that he was Chinese. It was clear from the expression on his face that he didn't understand what was being spoken about and what was being sold. He was tall and thin, a nervous type, perhaps a Virgo, as if he read books so as to look for accuracy and error. A book worm. He left the shop, then I went up to David Fogel.

"I am looking for a book."
"Who isn't looking for a book?"
"'HOME.'"
"'HOME'. Menashe Har Esh. Neshamah Press, no date listed, the two copies which were in the National Library were burned in the big fire thirty years ago. It seems it was a very limited printing. There is a certain demand for this book. Once I sold one copy, some years ago, or perhaps months ago, it turns up from time to time. I heard from a customer that professor David Yotuel,

of the University of Amman is doing research on this book and maybe it will be reedited by Keness Press in the near future, maybe you should go and speak with him."

"The University of Amman?"

"Rabat Ammon, near the Moab Mountains, takes fifty minutes on the Tel—Aviv Baghdad train. "

"I don't go to occupied cities."

"Not really occupied. We handed them over in the Baghdad—Kuneitra Agreement."

"Well, anyway, doesn't matter. Does the writer live in Jerusalem?"

"Used to live there. It's possible he's still alive, he should be about seventy, he was very young when he wrote most of his work, but he really didn't receive any sort of attention."

"Did you read the book?"

"Not really. I looked through it, I look through them all. It seems like a sort of philosophical novel, you know, like Javetz, Auster, Galneer — novels like that make me quite tired. I like philosophy and also novels, but separately..."

He creased up his forehead and continued, as though remembering something important.

"It was also theological, there was

something about the First Temple, it was written in code, like Nostradamus because at that time it was almost forbidden to talk about the Temple, just like during Nostradamus, prophecy was forbidden, there were manuscripts written with every other letter, giving instructions how to take control of the Temple Mount, with many mathematical equations, many dialogues. It was clear that the author was not sure of anything he said, each certitude brought another measure of doubt."

"Thank you for the details."

I went up to the mountain and looked out at the lights of the largest Arab city in Israel, Har Aviv, I saw the light rising above Jerusalem. There hasn't been rain for a long time, I said to myself out loud, and saw, behind me, the Chinese man in the shop saying 'Shalom' to me. I saluted him.

"Do you come here often?" he asked me.

"I come to this mountain, even though it's really a hill, I come to Mt. Har Afat to look for answers to questions, the height helps me think."

"Looking for a book?"

"Who isn't looking for a book?"

"Me, I've read them all. I'm now

reading them for the second time, because I don't have anything to do, my wife died two years ago, the children have left home, what do I have to do?"

I noticed that the man showed absolutely no sign of age, he could have been thirty or sixty, maybe that was because of his slanted eyes, his Chinese origin, or his smooth skin.

"Maybe you could help me, I'm looking for a book called HOME, have you read it?"

"HOME, certainly. That is, I'm sure that I didn't read it. No one has read it. But I'm sure that I read it. It's a book I'd want to find again, but no chance."

"That's not clear."

"It's a very strange book, a very few copies were printed. And, each copy is different from the next, not slightly different, rather each copy is essentially another book, I read two of the copies, each was different, and when I finished reading them I burned them."

"You burnt them?"

"Yes, because at the end the reader is asked to burn it, this really was convincing, so I burnt it, but even if I wasn't convinced, in the second book there were two pages of curses directed to the person who doesn't burn it. So, it turns out, pay attention, that the book must be in the house of someone who hasn't read it. Surprising, isn't it?"

"Yes, truthfully, I saw it in the house of someone who lives in Jerusalem, who said that the book is holy, belongs to a cult that believes in the religion of the state, the pages of the book were completely stuck together."

"I imagined all the copies of the book. For example, in one of them there would be curses to whoever was to read the book, in another, blessings for whoever
read the book, another tells about a lonely woman, and yet another about a man who searches for a woman he saw when he was fifteen years old, maybe all the books join together there. The smoke that rises from them, are you paying attention to what I'm saying, in the smoke that rises from the pages, like smoke which comes from the Torah scroll when it is burnt and one can see the letters rising to heaven, that's where the letters and images join one another."

"Amazing? ... tell me, do you believe in God?"

He looked at me with one eye and then the other, and said to me with authority. "Why not?"

"Why not?! ... I've never heard an answer like that."

"This was my father's answer, why not? What do you have to lose, you believe in God and that's it, what does it cost you?"

"In the same way you can say why yes."

"Why not?"

"Why not, or why yes?"

"You can say why yes, but it seems better to believe in God. You can pray to him when something troubles you, you cannot pray to a non—God when you are in trouble, you wouldn't pray to someone you don't believe in."

"Let's leave it for now, you'll never be a theologian. Tell me, did you burn more of Har Esh's books?"

"There are no more of his books, all of his books are HOME, maybe a hundred or two hundred books, no less than fifty, I've spoken with fifty people who have read it, no doubt they all remembered the book, and each of them talked about another book, no doubt about it, interest in HOME has fallen in the last ten years, well — for sure there are no copies left, or maybe Har Esh from time to time releases a book, another different and strange copy."

"And puts it in a used books store, maybe sells it, maybe he, himself, sells it."

"No one knows what he looks like ... it's possible, you know, entirely possible."

C
Jerusalem, winter, cold. The city looks like there's been a holiday, buildings dressed, as always, in stone, people walking back and forth. For some reason, as a way of distinguishing between other Israelis, their way of walking seems full of deep, fateful significance, as though each step is crucial to the future of humanity.

I slept in the Jacob Hotel and in the evening I drank Razin Brandy, the advertising slogan was 'Taller than Napolean' and in the picture you can see a tall bottle of Razin in contrast with Napoleon's short bottle, which, understandably relates to the favorite drinks of the two generals. From time to time books and articles appear with titles 'Who Killed Yaacov Razin?' or 'In whose interest was it not to save Razin?' with long debates over whether or not the murderer really murdered him, or was it a police guard who went with him to the hospital, or if his second in command was interested in his death, it's just that no one remembers the name of his second in command or any of the ministers of his government, all of whom died in different, strange beds. It all begins to be somewhat tiring. Reminiscent of Simone Bolivier in Venezuela — Razin Square, Jacob Boulevard, Jacob Hotel, Jacob Cake, Jacob Razin Shoe Store, Razin Hamburger Chain, why not?"

The followers, praying to the false gods of the Church of Peace in the name of Razin. seem to be especially dangerous. They believe that in name of Peace, one must overcome and kill the opposition, like during the Inquisition in the Middle Ages, like Christianity thousands of years ago.

I continue walking in Jerusalem and come to the Softic Church, its founder St. Bill originated the idea that God is a computer. He built a computer which improves itself by ten percent each year. People come to stare at this marvel, which, understandably, although I don't really know why this is so understandable, is in Jerusalem. The name of the program is God, and we are in the 70th God cycle, according to his believers when the 1000th program for God arrives, it can create an alternative world, and in this world the followers of St. Bill plan to live.

I wonder if it's possible to ask the computer about a book I'm looking for. They say that you can ask anything you want, the only thing is that each question costs 200,000 zuzim.

"Twenty year's salary?!" I'm amazed.

"But it'll have an answer for every question."

"Okay, I'll ask the editor."

A woman of about fifty waited for me outside and said: "I have an exact copy of the Softic program and I can do the work for you at a quarter of the price."

"I don't even have a quarter. Not even a third."

"A third is more than a quarter."

"Right. I don't even have a hundredth of it, but for a 100 zuzim, well, for a 100 zuzim, I can decide for myself."

"Okay, then come," she said, smiling slyly.

She looked very good, like a divorced woman who has managed to become independent after her husband had choked her. Dressed in the best Thai fashion, with expensive Indonesian shoes.

Those Softics think that they are the only ones who know the truth, sort of Messianic, you know, I copied the program, and in God 1000 it is impossible for a computer to built an alternative world, an alternative world can only be constructed through human imagination, they must forget about it, you can build another world, I can, but not the Softic, because they think that wisdom is in a machine and not in the most perfect creation of the universe, the human being, I haven't talked about this with anyone for a long time, my name is Zohara, from the Zohar language."

'You really are brilliant, very brilliant."

"Also stormy," she laughed, "Jerusalem makes me completely crazy, I am not at all a Jerusalemite, that's what they're called now, to be a Jerusalemite is a sort of special religion, here, there's a church on every corner, Scientology, Westernology, the Afula church, reformers who argue all the time with the reformists, never able to understand the difference between them, there are Conservatives, also the Serbic church was established here, you see, that's the Prophet's Street over there, and besides that you can see someone, what is someone, everyone, we are all prophets, for 2 zuzim, 2 zuzim, who will prophecy your future, for the entire country, even for your mother—in—law, I go crazy here, maybe I'll go back to Ashkelon, at least it's a city with a sea."

"Ashkelon was destroyed from an earth accident, an earthquake caused by underground vehicles, a gigantic computer that lost it's way, called the perpetual seeker, a cute name for a computer, there's no computer any more, also no Ashkelon, are you an Ashkelonite?"

"Actually my parents were born in Blazone, a small settlement near the Euphrates, it also disappeared, it was the most Eastern Jewish settlement 20 years ago, everything has disappeared in this world except for Jerusalem."

"Except for Jerusalem?"

"Except for Jerusalem, it seems impossible to make this city disappear, we've arrived, it's here, let's go up."

We went up to the third floor, on the way she asked what I was looking for.

"A book."

"Yes, that's clear, who's not looking for a book."

"'HOME' by Menashe Har Esh."

"Ah ... HOME who's not looking for a home.

"Have you heard of the book?"

"Sort of, a little, I'll tell you, I saw it in French and in English but not in Hebrew, in French it's called LA MAISON DE DIEU and in Spanish CASA EN FUEGO, why different names, I don't know, something else that's strange is that his name in Latin is not separated HARESH, one word, I don't know why, I saw them at friends abroad, but never in Hebrew."

"Well, let's ask the computer."

Very soon we received the answer from the God likeness: Menashe Har Esh, Home, Letter Publications, 1996, Jerusalem. Unknown number of copies, appears to be less than 200, book about the Holy Temple? unclear, appears to be a novel, no copies in the National Library.

"What is 1996?" I asked her.

Until recently, twenty or thirty years ago, they used to count the years from the birth of Jesus, the Jew from Nazareth."

"The Jew from Nazareth, what was so important about his birth?"

"His birth — not so much, his death was important, that's what his followers who were called Christians, believed, since Jesus was from Nazareth, they believed that he was

God who had arrived in the form of a human being and landed on earth, so they counted the years from his birth."

"What happened to this way of counting, to the Christians?"

"Thirty—five years ago, a method for examining the past was discovered, called the Memory of the Stones. One could take a stone and radiate from it everything that happened during the Stone Age, this is a very expensive process, however someone had enough money to prove the existence of Jesus that was, at that time, a very controversial subject. They discovered that Jesus did not exist, he never lived, not in Jerusalem and not in Nazareth."

"What? Did he want to see God, even stones can't remember something like that."

"I never thought of that."

In the meantime the computer came up with a number of facts about Har Esh. Menashe Har Esh: wrote five books, four books of poetry and one of prose, in Israel he hardly had success even though he had a few good critical reviews, his major publication was in France (today,western Galia) which is in Europe and in Tejas, a state in North America (the former United States). Maybe he lives in Europe now. His last credit card charge was listed in the city of Toulon five months ago.

"Toulon?"

"It's in Belgium."

"Is that far away?"

"Very far, I don't know if it's possible to go there, one has to go through the Black Rain region, it can kill a person if you aren't familiar with an alternative route, however I don't think one can get there a simple way."

The computer continues:

Toulon: a city at the foot of the Mediterranean Sea, an area that has suffered catastrophe. There are rumors that the city is still functioning however it doesn't seem possible to go there. Or to leave. Maybe with the hydraulic helicopter. But, it's not recommended.

"Once I flew there in a helicopter of that kind and it wasn't a pleasant experience. They say that it has side effects. Nothing happened to me but they say that it can even cause impotency and infertility, I wouldn't go on one."

"I wouldn't either, don't worry."

"Do you have where to sleep?"

"I'm staying in a small hotel not far from here."

We went to her room.

"You can sleep here if you want."

"And your husband?"

"Ah ... Moshe, I don't think he would care, if he even comes home in the next month or so, there are husbands who disappear for hours, he disappears for months, then he returns and asks if I've made lentil soup as though nothing has happened."

"Jerusalem ..."

"Moshe ..."

"Good, yes, yes, I very much would like to sleep here. The idea pleases me, you please me, our chance meeting pleases me. I'm going to stay here."

"I am also pleased."

I went to the hotel to bring my things and a traveler who saw me went with her to the house, gave me free advice, just like so much advice I received in Jerusalem: "Be careful — this adulteress will take you astray."

I said thank you and returned with my small suitcase.

I was very tired and went to sleep.

In the evening, after I had fallen asleep she asked a question about the book on the supernet and when I awoke there were a few answers which were no different from those I had received up until now, except for one.

"Hello, I am Menashe Har Esh, the author who wrote 'HOME'.

"Hello, my name is David Koresh and I am looking for your book because I am writing an article for the Modi'in Paper. Can you help me? First of all, I am concerned that perhaps you are not Menashe Har Esh, maybe you are someone else."

"Maybe you are someone else, maybe you aren't David Koresh, maybe you are Simcha Ben Balul, maybe you are Menashe Har Esh, maybe you wrote 'HOME'",

"why not?"

" I suggest you not ask questions like that if you don't want me to disappear from the line forever."

My concern didn't leave me, so I decided that I had nothing to lose so I continued with my questions.

"When did you write the book 'HOME'?"

"I haven't yet finished it. I'm writing it now."

"I found one copy of the book. How is it that you didn't write it?"

"I wrote it and didn't write it, that is, there were a few earlier editions, they weren't important, I'm bringing out a new edition very soon, or perhaps a first edition, 'HOME' is a book that is constantly changing, it changes from year to year, it changes from reader to reader, it changes from copy to copy."

"Where do you live?"

"In Austin, in the free republic of Tejas, Viva Tejas!!"

"Why so far away?"

"Far? ... far from what? Far from Mars, you are also the same distance from Mars, and also from Jupiter if you don't mind. We are both the same distance from Jupiter."

"From Jerusalem."

"Exactly the same distance, you are as far from Austin as I am from Jerusalem, to the millimeter."

"Is it true that you left Jerusalem because your book didn't succeed? Is it true that 'HOME' is to be published in French and English?"

"No, my books did succeed, there was even one reader who understood it, and this is great success in today's world, who has time to read a book with Supernet, with all the home computers, and a book in hard cover, that is hard to digest as a hard—boiled egg. Yes, the word 'HOME' appears in two books in French and Spanish, however, it's not the same book. In addition, no book can be the same as 'HOME', if you haven't understood this until now you are a lost case."

"I certainly am lost, the more I look for your book, the more lost I am. The more I know about it the more lost I am, could you send me a copy of the new edition?"

"Ah ... there won't be any change since the entire new edition will be one copy, maybe two, no chance, you'll have to look for it yourself, this copy certainly will not remain with me, it will be sent to some place, randomly, maybe to you, who knows, maybe add your name to the list of people interested in my work."

David Koresh, 95 Parsim Street, Modi'in, 5845/668, Israel.

"Okay, you're in."

"Could you tell me what 'HOME' is about?"

"No."

"Why not?"

"Because I don't know either."

"How old are you?"

"70 years old."

"Are you planning to return to Jerusalem?"

"I am planning to die in Jerusalem."

"Thank you."

She sat behind me all the time, listening in

on our conversation.

"So talkative", she said, "Do you want breakfast?"

"Why do you think that, maybe it's him, pretending to be Menashe Har Esh."

"It's no great honor."

"So if it is him, he's also talkative, a chatterbox."

Well, before I eat breakfast, I want to say to all my readers whose names I don't mention, that is what I requested, if I mention his name, or any other name instead of your name, immediately you will be identified, and you are a very familiar personality in Jerusalem.

"Okay, so tell them."

"Here — I said it."

"But, in any event, I could continue asking questions, maybe you would benefit from it."

"Look, the story went this way, at least that's what they say: My grandfather, or his father, it's not important, it was during the time of the plague in the city of Bensahwen where he was born, the cholera plague, he went into one of the large rooms of the house, before doing so he heard a scream. This was such a fatal plague that people went on their own to the cemetery because there was no one to bury them. He heard the scream and decided to close up the room, and it was not opened again for the entire time of the plague. Even some years after the plague was over, after five years or something like that, he dared to enter the room ... and then fell ill with cholera, he was sick for weeks then finally recovered."

"What's the connection?"

"I don't know, but many times when I don't have an answer, when a woman asks me a question and I feel like I must answer her, then I remember something about my family, it is something that I can't control, isn't that an interesting story?"

"There are a million stories like that one."

"Yes, all the million stories like that are interesting."

Jerusalem will pull you to visit each church, sect and religion, very soon you'll forget the very reason why you came. 'HOME' turned into a background for my constant discovery in the city, during cold sunny days, winter days which bore no resemblance to Modi'in. A different planet. At the beginning I was surprised that every person had something to say about 'HOME. It was as if everyone knew about it, but no one had read it, everyone had heard about it, from a father, an uncle, or a literature class. I didn't even find one person who had read the book. All these details eventually stopped interesting me, they also turned into a search for the answer to the significance of life, or sometimes just for the answer. As the preacher of the Spin church said: "Everyone looks for the answer but no one knows the question." This type of sentence stays engraved in your mind for years, maybe until your death. Really, what is the question? Does God exist? Yes or no, does this really solve something in our life, does God interfere in the workings of the world? This answer or any other doesn't offer a solution to our unrelenting existential pain, even if people tell you that this is so and or that we don't suffer from the same illness, from the same spiritual wanderings.

We should stop for a bit in front of an interesting church, the chemical church, constructed just 5 years ago, after the big plague, and after the government decided to impose rules that anyone wanting to use a chemical medicine must have the approval of a homeopath, must make sure that the homeopath is a reliable person. There are rumors about homeopaths who readily give permission in exchange for a bribe and other benefits. This is what the preacher said: "These homeopaths cause harm to our right to prevent our own pain even if it brings about a less difficult death. No one can prevent us from using antibiotics, even if proved that this leads to plagues, even if proof is doubtful, there were plagues before the use of antibiotics, plagues before the use of immunization, it is possible that antibiotics and immunization prevented some plagues, it's almost been 50 years, from the polio outburst till the outbreak of Aids there were good years, all sorts of chemical medicines were used, the homeopaths, with a strong lobby of homeopathic pharmaceutical companies profiting thousands of percentages that control those in power, convince them to accept laws which would cutback this wonderful medicine, 200 years of research down the drain because of politicians who do not understand anything about medicine, who are bribed to legislate bad laws. Long live antibiotics! Long live cortisone! Long live chemistry!"

I have repeated these things exactly as they were said, and they are recorded. I gave the cassette to the police since I think that there is more than a hint of rebellion, that no one will be surprised if in two years a crazy, frustrated individual doesn't turn up to murder the President of the Country."

D

The editor looked at me and at the same time looked at the diskette I handed him, placed his hand on top of his bald head, said "sit down", again looked at me, I thought he was going to fire me, something that would be much better for me since I didn't have the strength to leave the paper because it was comfortable and profitable, but that's what I really wanted to do.

"You have an interesting journalistic style, it reminds me of a number of books from the last generation, Ben Zimra, Auster, Libly, Benarroch, that kind of newspaper journalism is actually interesting."

"Auster? That tells me something, I heard that name before, but I haven't ever read one of his books."

"Doesn't matter, what bothers me in this article, is that we are left without 'HOME', and without Menashe Har Esh, maybe you should go to Austin to look for him."

"Go to Austin? ... that's really far, and besides I'm not sure at all that it's him, and I wrote that."

"There's good music there, you'll love it."

"I don't like music."

"It's hot there, good weather, not many clouds."

" I know, I know. My wife is interested in their music, but you are hiding the fact that it is very dangerous to get there, you have to travel through forbidden lands, and we're only talking about a book, and about a half—forgotten author, anyway it doesn't seem that there is very much interest in the book, who is interested in books today with the exception of editors and journalists, books are passé."

"Books are passé... where did you learn that word, they stopped using it fifty years ago, besides it's not even a Hebrew word. It's Galic."

"It is? I didn't know that, my grandfather used it all the time, he wasn't from Western Galia at all, once he went to Oran for a year or two, during the time of the Spanish Civil War, you remember, Jews, Moslems, Christians, but I think that Galic was also spoken in Morocco."

"Do you know what, leave it alone, maybe you should go to live in Jerusalem, and be our correspondent there for a year or so, write a few in—depth articles."

"A surprising suggestion, surprising suggestion."

"It surprises me too."

"I'll think about it."

My wife didn't agree, however I knew that I would go. In fact, I asked her but I knew that my decision had already been accepted, I couldn't refuse Jerusalem, a city connected with the future, a city in which the past is the future. At that very moment I didn't realize to what extent, I didn't know where I would find myself ten months later.

"The last thing that my grandfather told me, I was thirteen years old," I told her, "it was about the housekeeper he had in Morocco, her name was Fatima, she was very loyal to him and his younger brothers, he always remembered her. Loyal, what does it mean to be loyal, she also taught them by spanking them, it was acceptable then, but less than his mother did, one day she went with her husband to Belgium, and from there to a country that no longer exists today, she found work there, that's what happened to the

African countries at that time, they were freed from colonialism, the Western rule, then they began to look for cheap labor, a type of sophisticated labor, one could say and afterwards when they saw that in Europe they could get citizenship they began to work in weaker countries, were paid pennies. This was even more sophisticated work, until the Ayatollah Muhames came to power and expelled all the westerners from Arab countries and unified the Arabs... doesn't matter, so Fatima went to Belgium, one day after a number of years she appeared and brought for my mother a gift, a Tea set, and chocolate for the children. He would tell this story with tears in his eyes, that he didn't hug her, he was too embarrassed, maybe he was nine years old, and since then he hasn't seen Fatima."

"This is a good reason to go to Jerusalem, endanger your young family and our future."

"Believe me it's no safer here, you are a kilometer from the orange line, seven kilometers from the yellow line and five from the blue line."

"I don't look at lines anymore."

"Then how do you know that Jerusalem is more dangerous, from television? Do you believe the television?"

"That's what everyone says."

"Since when do you believe everyone and not me? I was there, it's very safe there, you'll see, come and see."

"I'll never go to Jerusalem, the city of rituals. That's not why my grandfather struggled, to remove the stupid rituals from the Jews. I belong to sane folks, not to mad people like you."

"Sane?"

"Yes, sane, you are crazy to go to a place where there's a synagogue on every corner, a church or a mosque where people get killed everyday."

"My grandfather told me that in Morocco people weren't killed because of their religion, and that's a fanatical Arab Moslem country. It's only here that everyone is killed because of your holy secularism."

"I've never heard you talk this way before."

"That's right. It's true that Jerusalem changed me. It's not just the book or working at the paper. I don't know, all these stones, the temple, the Temple Mount, the Softic church, the Mosque, they all pulled me back to my grandfather's stories, you haven't succeeded in secularizing me, it's as though my roots are too deep, too entrenched, as though the smell of olive oil calls me to come back, or the smell of my mother's milk, that's my roots, not purposeless secular Modi'in."

"Have you found a purpose in those religions?"

"I really don't know what I found, but I did find something."

"David, you didn't just leave Modi'in, you also left me, in your thoughts you left me some time ago."

"Maybe I am moving away from you, but I feel that you'll come after me, it's just a matter of time. Your daughter, our daughter, will bring you once again to me and Jerusalem. That's where we belong."

"If I were you I wouldn't be so sure of that, or of your feelings."

E

Every two weeks I sent in an article. 'HOME' turned into a passing memory. At the beginning I talked with my wife on the phone. I told her it was pleasant in Jerusalem. I tried to convince her to come but she didn't even visit me, until I finally stopped making suggestions. I won a prize for the article on the Sekhel Church, also known by the name of the Intellect Church. I became a well—known journalist and offers began to arrive from other newspapers, but all the writings on the churches simply increased my desire to know more about my place in the world.

All this will be cut short or skipped over suddenly when I arrived one winter morning to the book store in Jerusalem and saw the window full of copies of 'HOME' by Menashe Har Esh.

"Shalom," the female book seller said, "We are happy that you came to sign your books."

"Sign?"

"Yes, you're Menashe Har Esh, aren't

you?"

"Me?"

"Ah, maybe there is a mistake, but you look so much like the photograph on the back cover of the book." She showed it to him.

"That is really me."

I looked at the book, I saw my writings, my story.

"I really did write it, did I sleep for so long?"

I looked at my hands which always indicate age. They were the hands of a man of seventy years old.

"Seventy years old!"

"Yes, Sir, we've arranged a table for you, people will surely be coming soon."

"A table!"

I took a book and went out into the cold air. I was afraid to turn back toward the store, be old once again, but my hands didn't return to young skin, I ran, but my running had become slow and clumsy, I thought to myself that an old man of seventy running is as ridiculous as a poet who reads his poems at a literary evening or a journalist who tries to convince his editor to publish an article. I came to my favorite coffee shop 'The Hot Espresso'. I sat down, once again I opened the book 'HOME' written by Menashe Har

Esh, on the first page there was a signed inscription: "To my friend, David Koresh, without you this book would not have been published." Again I turned the pages, there was not one word of my writings on Jerusalem. Not even one sentence was familiar to me. At that moment I knew that I was starting a new religion. The waitress asked what I wanted.

I answered: "This can't be the end. This cannot be the end."

"That's right," she said. "It's true, this really is not the end."

Contents

HOME 3

THE HAND OF CIRCUMSTANCE 17

B 27

WITH HIS WIFE AT HOME 31

C 41

D 57

E 63

Made in the USA
Las Vegas, NV
21 June 2023